HAL•LEONARD

Pro Vocal®
BETTER THAN KARAOKE!

WOMEN'S EDITION   VOLUME 29

Torch Songs

T0056170

ISBN 978-1-4234-3192-3

HAL•LEONARD®
CORPORATION
7777 W. BLUEMOUND RD. P.O. BOX 13819 MILWAUKEE, WI 53213

Visit Hal Leonard Online at
www.halleonard.com

Angel Eyes

Words by Earl Brent
Music by Matt Dennis

Bewitched

from PAL JOEY

Words by Lorenz Hart
Music by Richard Rodgers

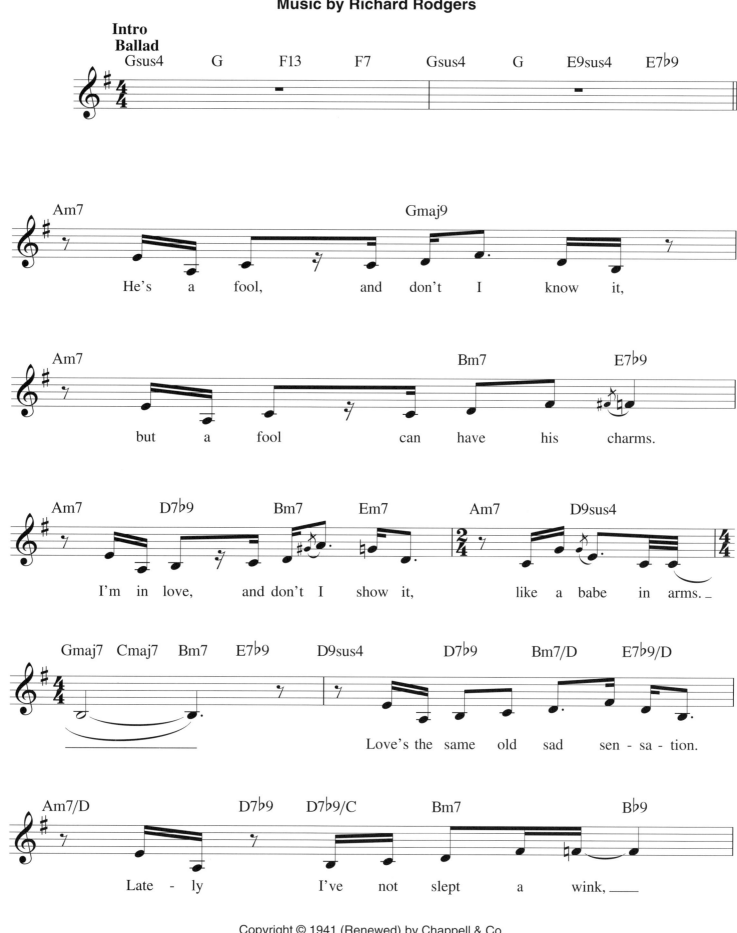

would-n't sleep _____ when love _____ came and __ told me __ I _____

_____ should-n't sleep. _____ Be - witched, both - ered and

be - wil - dered _____ am I. _____

Bridge

_____ Lost my heart,

but what of it? _____ He is cold, I _____

_____ a - gree. He _____ can __ laugh, ___ but

I love it, al - though __ the laugh's _____ on _____

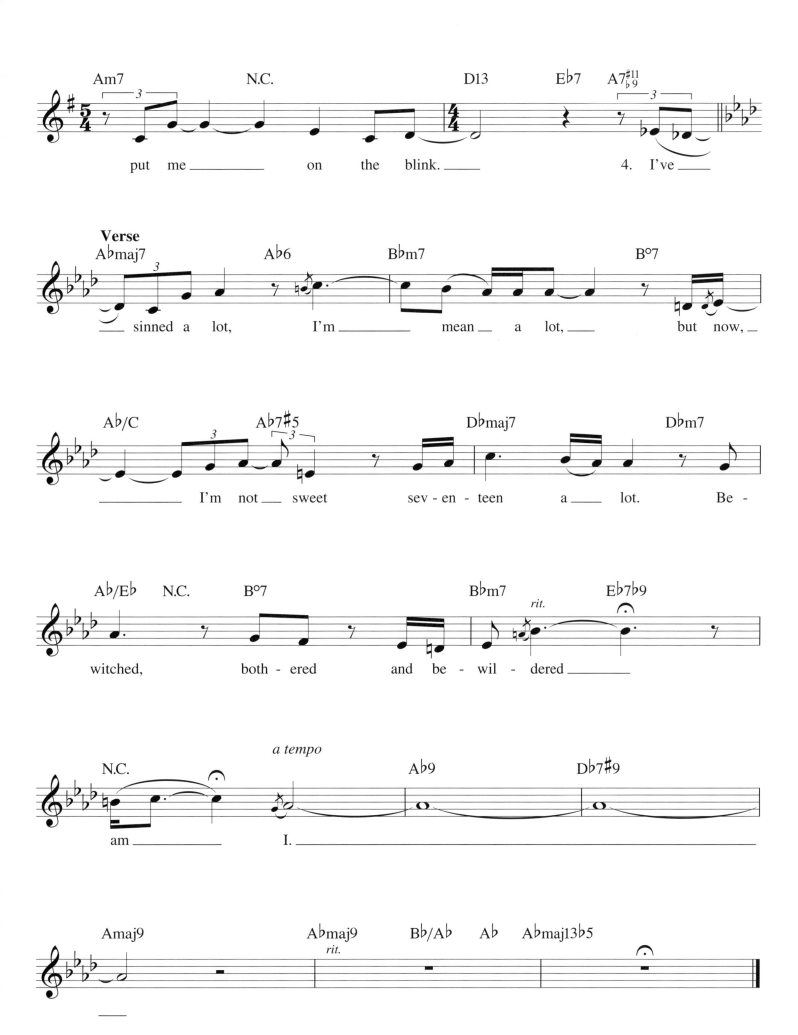

Can't Help Lovin' Dat Man

from SHOW BOAT

Lyrics by Oscar Hammerstein II
Music by Jerome Kern

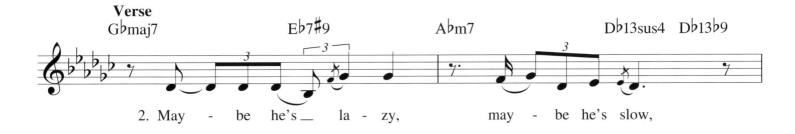

Verse

2. May - be he's __ la - zy, may - be he's slow,

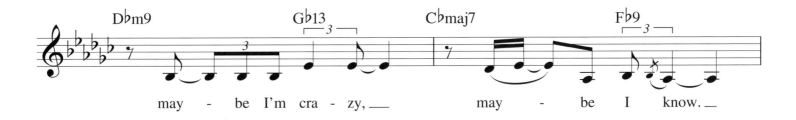

may - be I'm cra - zy, __ may - be I know. __

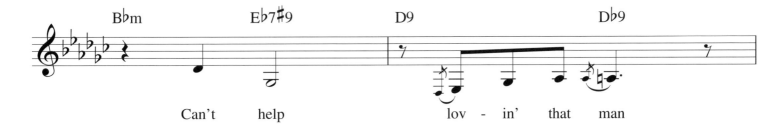

Can't help lov - in' that man

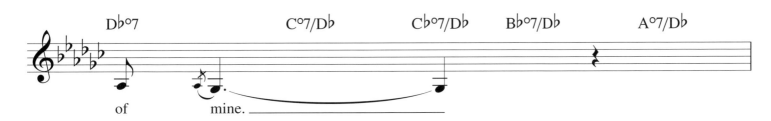

of mine. __

When __

Bridge

he __ goes a - way,

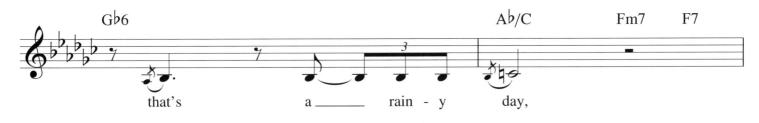

that's a __ rain - y day,

way,

that's _____ a rain - y

day,

but when he comes back, the day is

Ballad tempo

fine. The sun will shine. _____

Verse

3. He can stay out as late _____ as can _____ be. _____

_____ Home with-out him ain't no home _ for me. _____

Can't _ help _ lov - in' that man _____ of _____

mine.

I Concentrate on You

from BROADWAY MELODY OF 1940
Words and Music by Cole Porter

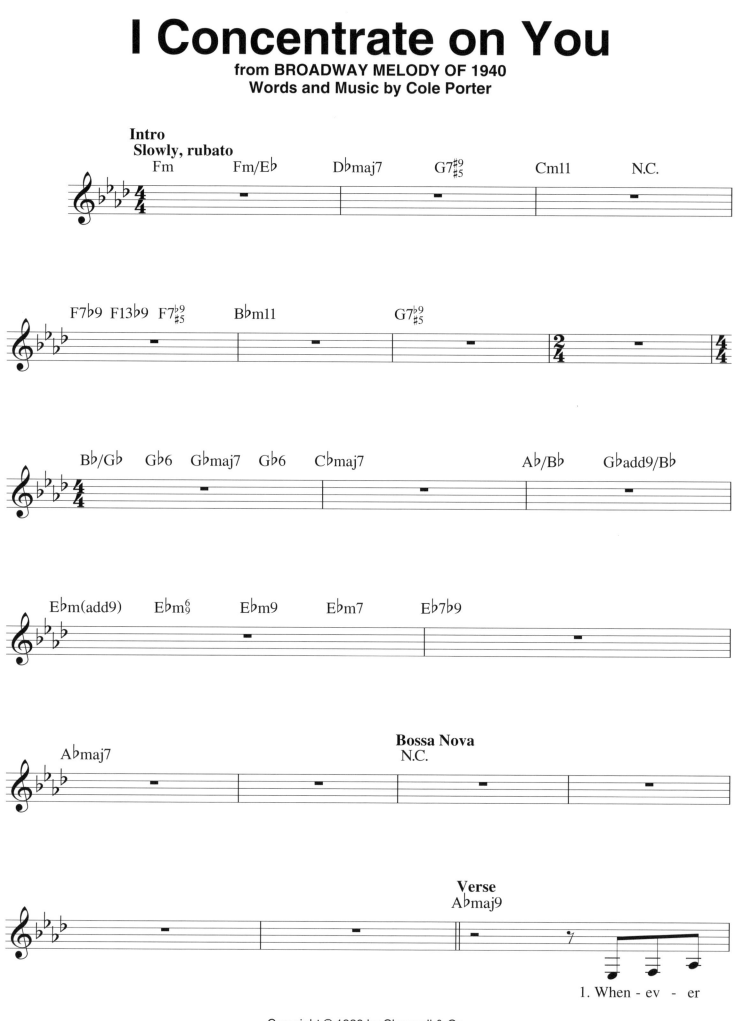

the wise _____ men say ___ to us _____

that love's young ___ dream _____ nev - er comes ___ true, _____

___ to prove that _____ e - ven

wise men can be _____ wrong, _____ I

con - cen - trate on _____ you. _____

Outro

Ooh.... _____

It Never Entered My Mind

from HIGHER AND HIGHER

Words by Lorenz Hart
Music by Richard Rodgers

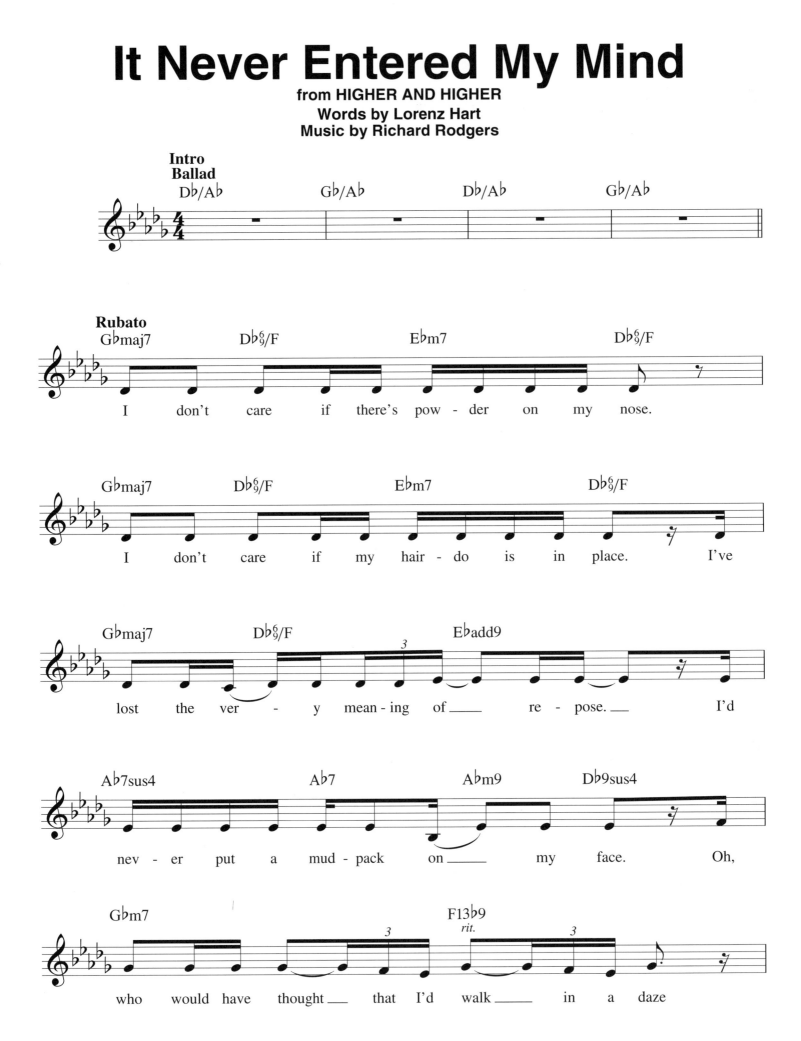

that   if   you   scorned   me,   I'd   sing   a   maid   -   en's

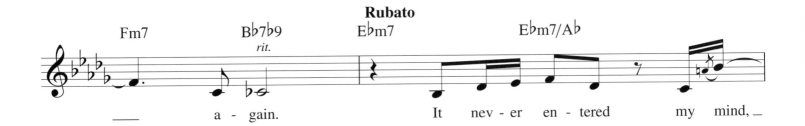

prayer ____   a - gain   and   wish   that   you ____   were   there ____

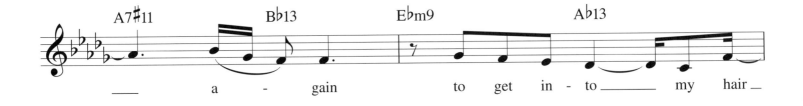

____   a   -   gain   to   get   in - to _____   my   hair ____

Rubato

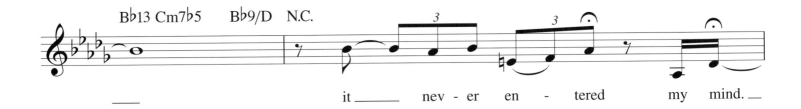

____   a - gain.   It   nev - er   en - tered   my   mind, ____

____   it _____   nev - er   en - tered   my   mind. ____

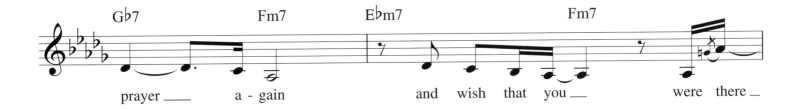

A Sunday Kind of Love

Words and Music by Louis Prima, Anita Nye, Stan Rhodes and Barbara Belle

to keep me warm _____ when _____ Mon - days ___

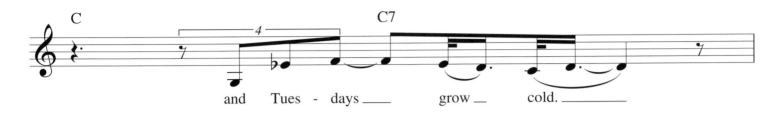

and Tues - days ____ grow ___ cold. _____

Love ___ for all my ___ life _____ to have ___

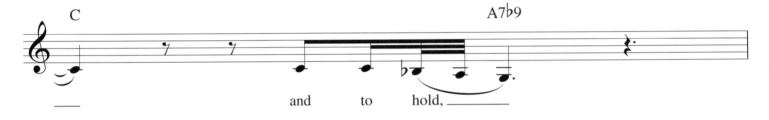

___ and to hold, _____

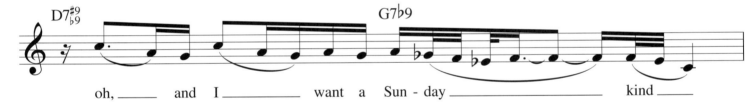

oh, _____ and I _____ want a Sun - day _____ kind ___

of love. _____ Oh, _____ yeah, _____

___ yeah, ___ yeah. _____ I don't want a _____

Outro

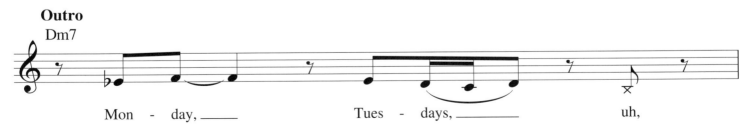

Mon - day, _____ Tues - days, _____ uh,

You Don't Know What Love Is

Words and Music by Don Raye and Gene De Paul

Time After Time

from the Metro-Goldwyn-Mayer Picture IT HAPPENED IN BROOKLYN
Words by Sammy Cahn
Music by Jule Styne

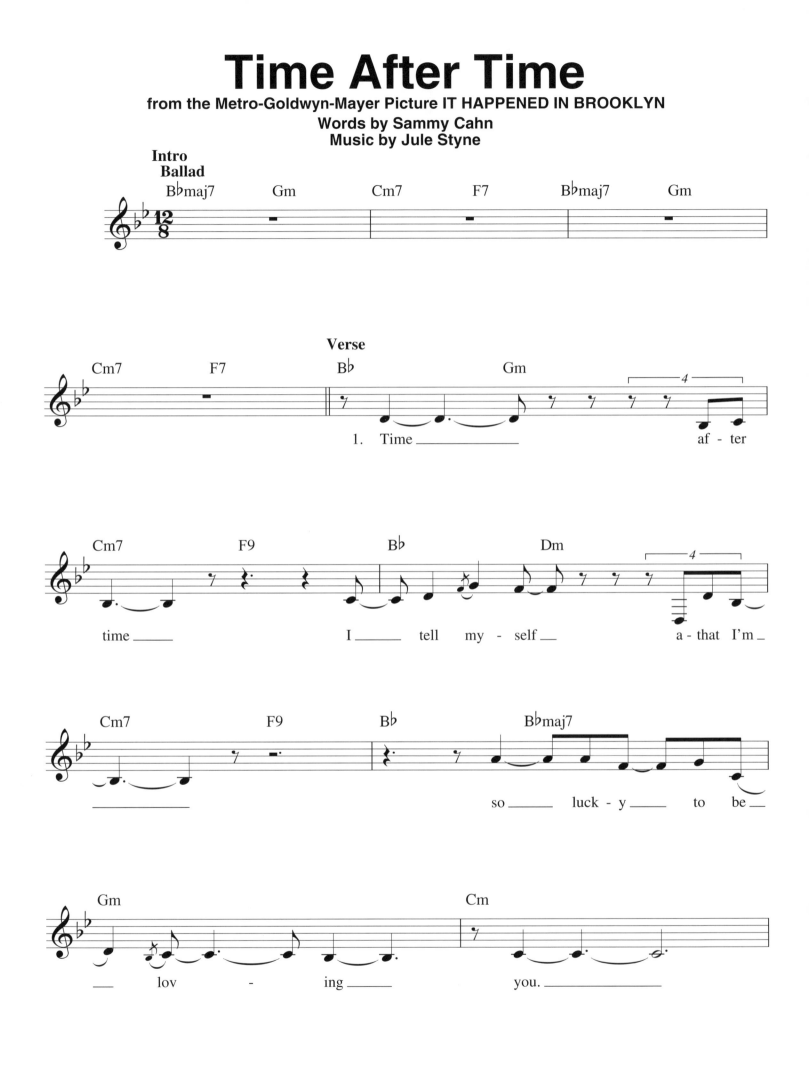

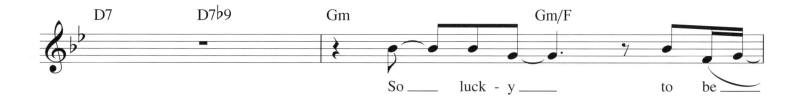

So ____ luck - y ____ to be ____

____ the one you run ____ to _____

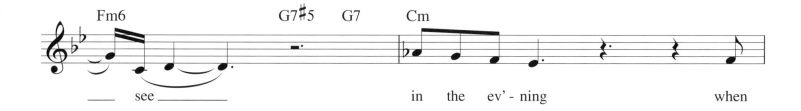

____ see _____ in the ev' - ning when

the day _____ is through. ____

Verse

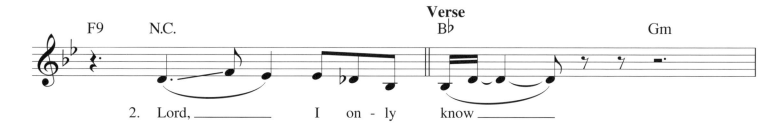

2. Lord, _____ I on - ly know _____

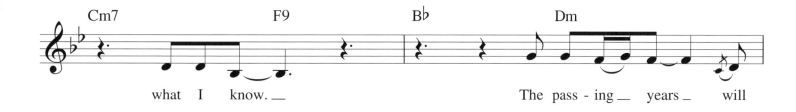

what I know. ____ The pass - ing ___ years ___ will

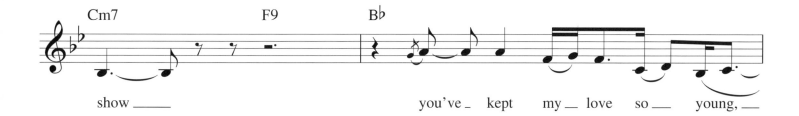

show ____ you've __ kept my __ love so __ young, __

37

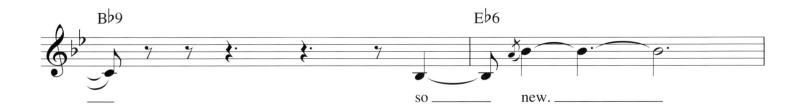

so _____ new. _____

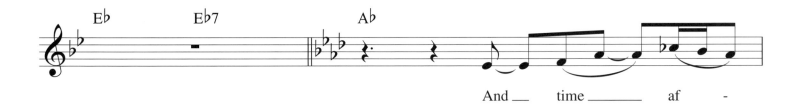

And __ time _____ af -

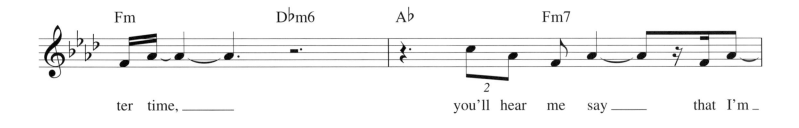

ter   time, _____   you'll hear   me   say _____   that I'm __

_____   so _____ luck - y,   so ____ luck - y   to be   lov -

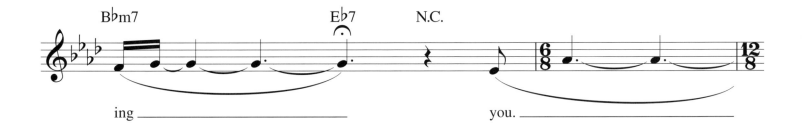

ing _____   you. _____

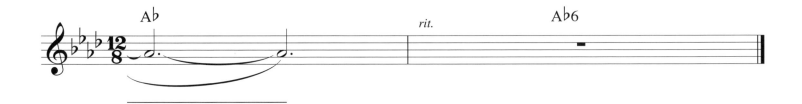